Editing Fiction Containing Gender-Neutral Pronouns

Louise Harnby

First published in the UK in 2021 by
Chartered Institute of Editing and Proofreading
Apsley House
176 Upper Richmond Road
London
SW15 2SH

ciep.uk

Copyright © 2021 Chartered Institute of Editing and Proofreading

ISBN 978 1 915141 07 1 (print)
ISBN 978 1 915141 06 4 (PDF ebook)

All rights reserved. No part of this publication may be reproduced or used in any manner without written permission from the publisher, except for quoting brief passages in a review.

The moral rights of the author have been asserted.

The information in this work is accurate and current at the time of publication to the best of the author's and publisher's knowledge, but it has been written as a short summary or introduction only. Readers are advised to take further steps to ensure the correctness, sufficiency or completeness of this information for their own purposes.

Development editing, copyediting and proofreading by Margaret Hunter, Luke Finley, Sophie Playle, Nick Taylor, Ian Howe and Michelle Bullock.

Typeset in-house
Original design by Ave Design (**avedesignstudio.com**)

Contents

1 |	Introduction	1
2 |	Exploring pronouns and terminology	2
3 |	What fiction editors need to understand	3
4 |	Personal pronouns: who's in control?	4
	A traditional approach to pronouns	4
	A conscious-language approach to pronouns	5
5 |	What can be known and what must be revealed	6
	Normative pronoun use	6
	Conscious-language pronoun use	7
6 |	Why narrative viewpoint matters	8
	Narrative style	8
	Viewpoint characters	9
	Non-viewpoint characters	10
	Omniscient narrators	11
7 |	Characters reporting what they can't know	12
	Why dropped viewpoint is problematic	12
	Single-pronoun universes in third-person limited narrations	13
	Multiple-pronoun universes in third-person limited narrations	14

8 |	Identity-based pronouns and viewpoint problems	16
	Example 1: Normative multiple-pronoun universe	16
	Example 2: Reimagined single-pronoun universe	17
	Example 3: Reimagined multiple-pronoun universe	18
	Example 4: Reimagined multiple-pronoun universe	20
9 |	Are identity-based pronouns overwhelming readability?	21
10 |	Acknowledging gender identity without pronouns	22
11 |	Examples of third-person pronouns	23
12 |	Tracking characters' pronouns	25
13 |	Can fiction include a mixture of gendered and gender-neutral pronouns?	26
14 |	Should writers include explanations?	27
	Centring character	27
	Centring marginalisation	28
	Pronunciation and information	28
15 |	Summing up	29
16 |	Resources	30
Appendix |	Summary of narrative viewpoint styles	32
About the author		38

1 | Introduction

Editing fiction with gender-neutral pronouns isn't as simple as ensuring consistency and spelling. In certain narrative styles, character identity has to be revealed rather than assumed. This guide examines what to watch out for.

Readers are asked to bear in mind that this resource doesn't seek to give primacy to any one pronoun over another, gendered or not. Rather, it aims to support editors working on (or deciding whether to work on) fiction that contains gender-neutral pronouns.

2 | Exploring pronouns and terminology

Perhaps you're already familiar with the many pronouns available beyond 'she', 'he' and 'it', 'one' and 'they'.

How about 'hir', 'per', 'xe' and 'thon'? There are many more. Take a look at the following online guides as a starting point.

- Pronouns 101: **queerlittlefamily.co.uk/pronouns101**
- Preferred gender pronoun/personal pronouns: **wou.edu/wp/safezone/pronoun**

Safe Zone Project's online glossary (**thesafezoneproject.com/resources/vocabulary**) is a useful place to explore definitions relating to identity and sexuality.

3 | What fiction editors need to understand

If we're to help our authors craft immersive fiction, there are three things we need to understand:

- who's in control of deciding the correct pronoun
- the difference between what can be known and what must be assumed until knowledge is revealed
- what narrative viewpoint is and how it's connected to assumption and revelation.

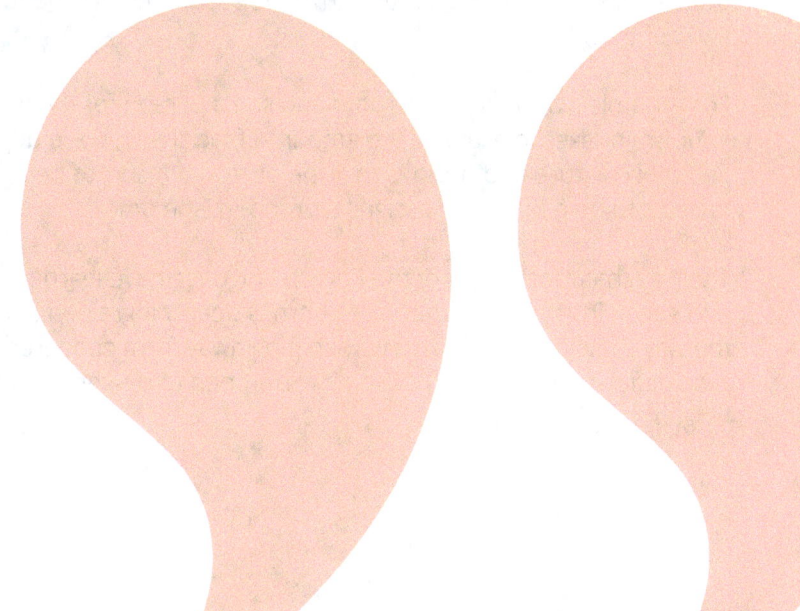

4 | Personal pronouns: who's in control?

Personal pronouns are substitutes for proper nouns. They enable us to write economically and avoid repetition. Their grammatical function is embedded deeply in the normative grammatical conventions of the English language.

- Some personal pronouns are gendered, for example she/her, he/him.
- Some are gender-neutral, for example they/them, we/us, I/me.
- Some people choose to use a combination, for example he/they.

A traditional approach to pronouns

Traditionally, these grammatical markers are *prescribed* according to what someone *perceives*. Audiovisual information and actions/behaviour give the viewer clues that align with normative assumptions around biology and gender.

For example, you walk into a room and see a person for the first time. Your brain takes in a larynx, the amount of facial hair, voice depth, height and musculature and decides that the person *appears* to be a woman or *appears* to be a man, and assigns a pronoun: she or he.

The way that most users of the English language have learned to write and speak from the day they were born is deeply ingrained and affects the way they *think*. And that's why shifting away from gendered pronouns is so difficult for many of us, even if we're open to de-gendering our language.

What's important to recognise here is that the personal pronouns are *prescribed by the perceiver*. They control which ones are being used. And that means that personal pronouns are dislocated from subjective identity – how the person being viewed experiences their own sense of self.

This approach **sidelines (or invisibilises) identity**.

A conscious-language approach to pronouns

When we think of pronouns with a conscious-language mindset, we allow the person being perceived, rather than the perceiver, to take control of their own pronouns.

Pronouns are just like religious beliefs, cultural relationships, emotional attachments, likes and dislikes, fears and hopes. They're not prescribed but chosen by each individual for themself.

Perhaps a person chooses 'they' for themself because it's a familiar pronoun, has been in use for hundreds of years as a singular gender-neutral pronoun, and is unlikely to be misspelled or mispronounced. Or perhaps 'per' is chosen because of the connection with the word 'person'.

Regardless, everyone has the right to choose how they want others to refer to them in the third person. What's important to bear in mind is that choices and preferences can only be known by others once they've been revealed in some way.

This approach **centres identity**.

5 | What can be known and what must be revealed

Normative pronoun use

When writing incorporates the *traditional* use of pronouns, gender identity and the words we use to reflect it aren't being challenged; they're not part of the story any more than the pronouns we assign to inanimate objects. Readers don't question these choices because they're considered standard. For example:

- An object with a flat surface and four legs at each corner is called a 'table' and the pronoun is 'it'.
- A construction of bricks with a roof on top is called a 'house' and the pronoun is 'it'.
- A person with a penis and a protruding larynx is traditionally called a 'man' and the pronoun is 'he'.
- A person with a vagina and breasts is traditionally called a 'woman' and the pronoun is 'she'.

Some information, however, must be revealed in order to be known:

- The table was owned by Auntie Mabel.
- The house is built where a medieval church once stood.
- The man is called Tom Brody.
- The woman is called Diane Desjardin.

Conscious-language pronoun use

When writing shifts into a *conscious-language space*, and traditional pronoun assignment is challenged such that identity is in play, the words 'man', 'woman', 'he' and 'she' cannot be known simply by looking at a character and how they behave, or by hearing their voice. These things must be revealed, just like Auntie Mabel's ownership of the table, because what can be perceived – larynxes, facial hair, voice depth, height, musculature – may or may not align with gender identity.

Yes, a character can still walk into a room and encounter another person who *appears* to be a woman or a man, and can assign a pronoun – even a gender-neutral one – but they can't be sure that it's the correct one because they're not in a position to know. Only once the person's true sense of self has been revealed to them can they be sure that the pronoun they assign is correct. Until then, the pronouns they use will be guesswork.

And that's where things can get very tricky in fiction because it affects narrative viewpoint.

6 | Why narrative viewpoint matters

Every novel has a narrator. The perspective of that narrator is referred to as narrative viewpoint. Who that narrator is will determine what can be reported to the reader.

Narrative style

Viewpoint is complicated – for writers and editors. Writers can use one or several narrative styles in a novel. For example:

- first-person limited
- first-person omniscient
- second person
- third-person limited
- third-person objective
- third-person omniscient.

There's a summary of the narrative viewpoint styles you're most likely to come across in commercial fiction, and their limitations, in the **Appendix**.

Skilled writers can blend narrative viewpoints even within a chapter or section by controlling the narrative or psychic distance between the reader and the viewpoint character or narrator.

Viewpoint characters

Viewpoint characters are those whose experiences drive a scene or chapter.

There can be more than one in a novel but to avoid confusion, writers and editors often recommend that each viewpoint character's narrative is separated by a section or chapter break.

It is viewpoint characters who report what's happening, and we have access to what they can see, hear, think, know and feel – their lived experience within the novel.

However, until another character's identity has been revealed to the viewpoint character, they have to make assumptions. The language they use to mitigate those assumptions will depend on where they sit on the conscious-language spectrum.

Viewpoint characters can narrate in the third person (as well as in the first person) and therefore use their pronoun of choice for themselves because it's theirs to choose and use.

Here's an excerpt from *The Ghost Fields* by Elly Griffiths (p67). Ruth is the viewpoint character.

> Ruth is slightly disconcerted to think that she has been the subject of discussion between Nelson and Clough. She always wonders what Nelson's colleagues think of her. Well, Judy's a friend, but the others – Clough, Tim and Tanya – they're a slightly unknown quantity.

If Griffiths had wanted to create a character whose pronoun is 'xe' rather than 'she', it would look like this:

> Ruth is slightly disconcerted to think that xe has been the subject of discussion between Nelson and Clough. Xe always wonders what Nelson's colleagues think of xer. Well, Judy's a friend, but the others – Clough, Tim and Tanya – they're a slightly unknown quantity.

Non-viewpoint characters

Non-viewpoint characters are those who the viewpoint character (and an omniscient narrator) – and therefore the reader – can see and hear. In *limited* narrative styles we know them only objectively. So if the viewpoint character knows intimate details about a non-viewpoint character because they've been friends for years, the reader can access that information too – via the viewpoint character.

However, if a non-viewpoint character is a stranger, the reader can't know anything about what they think or feel, including what their favourite food is, what their worst fear is, how they identify in terms of their religiosity or sexuality, or what their chosen pronouns are.

Instead, this information will have to be revealed – through dialogue or through information passed on by other characters who are in the know. And until that reveal occurs, the viewpoint character will necessarily make assumptions and mistakes, just like people do in real life.

It's therefore critical that editors working on novels containing characters with gender-neutral pronouns (and indeed gendered pronouns that don't align with birth-assigned sex) understand narrative viewpoint so that they can flag up occurrences of when the viewpoint character reports what they can't know.

Omniscient narrators

Omniscient narrators might be characters in a story or stand outside the novel.

For example, in Markus Zusak's *The Book Thief*, Death is the first-person omniscient narrator and also a character. Whereas in Cormac McCarthy's *The Road* the third-person omniscient narrator is external.

Omniscient narrators have access to every aspect of a story – all the characters' movements, thoughts, feelings ... and their correct pronouns!

If an omniscient narrator is doing the reporting, the only pronoun slips will necessarily be in the dialogue of characters who don't yet know what another's choices are.

7 | Characters reporting what they can't know

When viewpoint characters report what they can't know, authors are said to have **dropped viewpoint**, whereas when the narration is appropriately limited by what is properly known because it's been revealed, **viewpoint has been held** or is intact.

Imagine a fictional universe where no one makes mistakes, and every character gets every other character's pronoun right without being told that information.

It's possible that your author has created such a universe, and if they've used an omniscient narrator, they'll be able to pull off that scenario because omniscient narrators are godlike and know everything about everyone.

However, if they're writing in a third-person limited narration (in which the reporting is done by a viewpoint character), pronoun usage will need to be handled carefully in order to hold viewpoint.

Why dropped viewpoint is problematic

We can imagine ourselves as viewpoint characters because that's exactly how we live out our lives. We're not telepathic. We know exactly what's going on in our own heads but only know what's going on in other people's when they reveal it to us (or someone else does). That's why we make assumptions and mistakes.

When an author commits to writing one viewpoint character in a particular section of a novel but then gives readers access to a non-viewpoint character's internal experience, it stops us investing fully with the viewpoint character. Instead of immersing ourselves in the viewpoint character's experience so that we almost become them, live every moment with them, we bounce from one character's psyche to another, as if telepathy is in play. That's unrealistic and inauthentic, and it's often referred to as **head-hopping**.

Head-hopping rarely offers a good reader experience, and there's a risk the reader will think the prose is amateurish and poorly crafted. That can lead to negative reviews and lower sales. For the writer seeking representation from a literary agent, it's more likely to land them in the rejection pile. And so the fiction editor needs to be able to advise an author or publisher when viewpoint isn't being handled appropriately.

How easy it will be to hold viewpoint in a limited narrative viewpoint style while embracing gender-neutral pronoun usage will depend on whether the characters inhabit a single-pronoun or multiple-pronoun universe.

Single-pronoun universes in third-person limited narrations

Universes with only one universally accepted pronoun are easier to write and edit because there's no opportunity for a character to know what they can't know about pronoun choices.

Because there's only one pronoun – even if the author has opted for a gender-neutral one – it's no longer situated within the identity sphere. Instead, it's prescribed objectively to all characters, and performs a traditional function of grammatical economy, just a gender-neutral one.

Perhaps, for example, in this universe the third-person pronoun is 'ze'/'zir'/'zirs' (rather than 'she'/'her'/'hers' or 'they'/'them'/'theirs') regardless of a person's gender identity.

Multiple-pronoun universes in third-person limited narrations

Universes in which characters have the choice of different pronouns are trickier to write and edit when those pronouns are based on subjective identity rather than objective perceptions.

In that case, a character's pronouns must be learned by other characters, through enquiry of some sort – dialogue, a badge, a Twitter handle, a signature in a letter – if the author is to challenge normative ideas about pronouns without dropping viewpoint.

Until pronouns are learned they will be assumed, and that means the viewpoint character will invariably make mistakes – just like in the real world.

In Michael Sullivan's *Hollow World*, Ellis Rogers time-travels forward two thousand years into a world in which sex and gender have been phased out. Ellis is the viewpoint character and the narration style is third-person limited. In this excerpt, which I've added emphasis to, Ellis has recently arrived in the future only to discover a murder victim. In the final paragraph, he comes round after having passed out.

> "Everyone just stay back."
> "Darwin—has to be."
> "Anyone see the attack?"
> "No. I was the one who reported it—who requested help. We didn't see it, though. **They** were like that when we found **them**."
> "And you're part of the same group?"
> "Gale University—I'm leading a class in ancient history. We were on a field trip."
> "All right, you can do us a favor and just continue with that. Stay clear of this side of the park, okay?"
> "Is it really a Darwin?"
> "We don't know what we're dealing with yet, so please give us room."
> Ellis opened **his** eyes and found the blue sky, now decorated with pretty balls of white cotton. The light was different, the sun having moved well to the west so that the trees and farmhouse were casting long shadows. **His** chest was better. **He** could breathe again, yet everything else felt sore. (p46)

7 | Characters reporting what they can't know

Notice how Sullivan holds viewpoint by using dialogue to show the non-viewpoint character's prescription of the singular 'they' to describe Ellis. It's actually a mistake on the speaker's part, but a necessary one because they can't yet know Ellis's chosen pronoun. However, through Ellis's thought processes, which readers do have access to because he's the viewpoint character, we learn that he identifies as 'he'.

8 | Identity-based pronouns and viewpoint problems

The following examples show why fiction that challenges normative handling of pronouns and identity needs to be handled with care.

Example 1: Normative multiple-pronoun universe

In this excerpt, the narration style is third-person limited and Diane is the viewpoint character. This piece treats pronouns traditionally – they're gendered, based on objective experience and dislocated from identity. This approach is the one that many of us use in day-to-day speech. It's also in most of the books we read. And it's what many of us edit.

> The bell rang and Diane looked up. A stranger stood in the doorway. How the hell he'd got past security was anyone's guess. She smiled anyway.
> Tom Brody tipped his hat and wished he had a cigarette. The nicotine cravings were doing his head in.

There's a problem. Because Diane is the viewpoint character, the reader should be able to access only *her* thoughts and knowledge and what she can hear and see. The interior identity traits of the man in the doorway – his name and nicotine cravings – should be hidden to her and therefore to us. They need to be learned. Yet in the above example, they've been revealed by the author, not the viewpoint character. It's a viewpoint drop. Let's fix it:

> The bell rang and Diane looked up. A stranger stood in the doorway. How the hell he'd got past security was anyone's guess. She smiled anyway.
> The man tipped his hat. 'Tom Brody. Don't suppose you've got a cigarette, have you? The cravings are doing my head in.'

The dialogue allows the man to introduce himself and tell Diane (and readers) what's going on in his head. Aspects of his identity have been revealed in a manner that leaves viewpoint intact.

Notice, however, that pronouns are automatically prescribed by the viewpoint character based on what she sees and assumes. Gender identity, as something owned by the man, is erased.

This style of this writing approach is normative and so deeply ingrained in how we're used to using language that it would never be considered problematic in terms of viewpoint.

Example 2: Reimagined single-pronoun universe

In this excerpt, the narration style is still third-person limited and Diane is still the viewpoint character but the author has elected to partially challenge normative pronoun use by using one pronoun: 'ze'. Pronoun use is therefore now gender-neutral, though gender identity isn't being centred because a single pronoun is assigned to all characters regardless of their sense of self.

> The bell rang and Diane looked up. A stranger stood in the doorway. How the hell ze'd got past security was anyone's guess. Ze smiled anyway.
> The visitor tipped zir hat. 'Tom Brody. Don't suppose you've got a cigarette, have you? The cravings are doing my head in.'

All is well apart from the ambiguity around who's doing the smiling. To fix that, we could edit it as follows: 'Diane smiled anyway.'

This is the simplest scenario to edit because as long as the editor knows which pronoun the author wants to use, the editor can search for any anomalies without worrying about who the viewpoint character is and what they do or don't know.

Example 3: Reimagined multiple-pronoun universe

This is where things can get complicated. In the example below, one of the pronouns being used is familiar, but even so, the author is writing with a conscious-language mindset.

In this universe, there are multiple pronouns available, just as there are in British English, and characters have choices rather than their pronouns being prescribed by others. Still, viewpoint characters are limited by what they actually know.

The narration style is third-person limited and Diane is the viewpoint character.

> The bell rang and Diane looked up. A stranger stood in the doorway. How the hell ze'd got past security was anyone's guess. She smiled anyway.
> The visitor tipped zer hat. 'Tom Brody. Don't suppose you've got a cigarette, have you? The cravings are doing my head in.'

Is there a problem? It depends. Because Diane is the viewpoint character, she gets to use her own pronoun of choice – 'she' – because she knows her own gender identity and can report it. But what about the stranger? This person is a non-viewpoint character, which means readers don't have access to this person's sense of self – thoughts, feelings, beliefs, preferences, associations.

If Diane is someone who always does the best she can to avoid prescribing others with gendered pronouns, and her standard non-gendered default is 'ze', the text is in good shape and viewpoint is held.

If, however, she usually defaults to 'they', even though Tom zemself actually uses 'ze', it's a viewpoint drop because Diane doesn't yet know Tom's choice. And in that case, we could suggest the author consider the following:

> The door opened and Diane looked up. A stranger stood in the doorway. How the hell **they'd** got past security was anyone's guess. She smiled anyway.
> The visitor tipped **their** hat. 'Tom Brody. Don't suppose you've got a cigarette, have you? The cravings are doing my head in.'

Then the author would need to think about how they might enable Tom to reveal zer choice. It might happen soon; it might happen a little later on in the novel, perhaps in a conversation with a colleague who knows Tom, or perhaps because Tom overhears Diane referring to zem as 'they'. For example:

> 'I just met Tom Brody. Reckon they'll fit in well,' Diane said.
> She felt a tap on her shoulder and turned. Brody. Back already.
> 'It's ze, not he or they,' Brody said. 'Just letting you know.'

On the other hand, if the narrative arc is exploring a more significant disruption to Diane's mindset – someone who's on a journey of change – we might suggest something on the lines of the following:

> The door opened and Diane looked up. A stranger stood in the doorway. How the hell **he'd** got past security was anyone's guess. She smiled anyway.
> The man tipped **his** hat. 'Tom Brody. Don't suppose you've got a cigarette, have you? The cravings are doing my head in.'

And then later:

> 'I just met Tom Brody. Reckon he'll fit in well,' Diane said.
> She felt a tap on her shoulder and turned. Brody. Back already.
> 'It's ze, not he. Just letting you know.'
> She'd heard people use *they* in the singular but ze? That was a new one on her. Fair enough, though. She could go with that.

Example 4: Reimagined multiple-pronoun universe

The diligent editor needs to consider yet another complication. If the next chapter sets up Tom Brody as the viewpoint character, now we have access to zer interior space, which of course includes zer gender identity and chosen pronouns.

And so now Tom's third-person-limited narration will use 'ze'. However, ze knows nothing about Diane so won't know her choices until they're revealed. The author will need to have made a decision about the language choices Tom uses to describe others in the third person, and how this might shift as ze discovers more about the characters ze's interacting with.

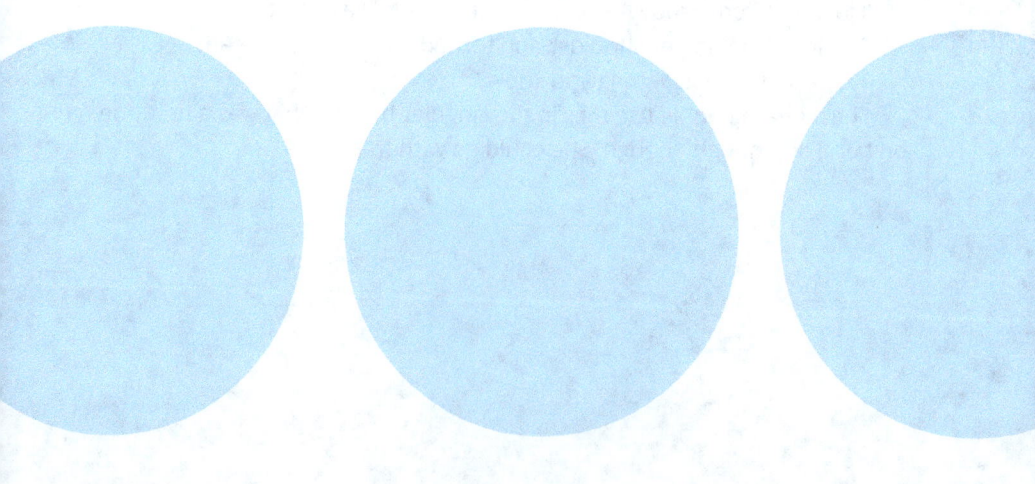

9 | Are identity-based pronouns overwhelming readability?

You should now understand that in third-person-limited narrations – which are common in fiction – as soon as pronoun use shifts from objective normative grammar (which doesn't require consideration of viewpoint) to subjective identity (which does), its role as a shorthand substitute for proper names loses its economy.

For that reason, some authors might opt for alternative pronouns that are gender-neutral but not located within identity consciousness.

Fiction editors need to bear in mind that such a choice might in itself be problematic and not serve the very community whose voices it wants to amplify.

> [I]n fiction, there is no need to cover over gender ambiguity because we should know what gender the characters are. Relegating [trans individuals] to gender-neutral usages is actually a form of erasure in that sense because it denies them the right to identify themselves the way they are most comfortable.
>
> SL Armstrong, 'Gender neutral pronouns in fiction'

Our authors, of course, are free to make their own decisions, and as with so much in the craft of professional editing and writing, there are multiple opinions and multiple preferences.

However, being a professional editor puts us in a position of privilege because we have an opportunity to educate our authors and publisher clients. That doesn't mean telling them what to do but rather guiding them on what the options are so that the decisions are informed and based on choice rather than ignorance.

10 | Acknowledging gender identity without pronouns

Editors can help their authors respect character identity and hold viewpoint by avoiding gender-neutral pronouns. Instead:

- repeat proper names
- use indefinite and definite articles.

In *Hollow World*, Michael Sullivan manages to avoid virtually all pronouns that relate to non-viewpoint characters by using these two techniques. It's a little clumsy at times but readable.

> **Pax** struggled. "No. It still won't work. It's frozen. I think the interaction with the other tunnel broke both of—oh, wait." **Pax** looked puzzled. "The lock is on this one. No one puts the lock on." Pax slid **a finger** across the surface of the device. (p326)
>
> "I can't get it to work," Pax cried, wiping the screen on the thigh of **the Amish pants**. "It's not the blood—it just won't work! It's broken like the other one." (p324)
>
> "What happened?" Ellis asked. "Why did Pax—why did you have to start living here?"
> "I don't know. **Pax** has never told me. I learned about it through mutual friends. **Pax** was in an emergency room under observation. No one knew what to do. What **Pax** needed was **Pax**—someone who could look inside and understand the demons. But there is only one **Pax**. Still, I couldn't let…I volunteered to move in, to watch and protect **Pax**. I'd do anything, you understand—anything, only I'm not **Pax**. I can't do the magic, and I watched the depression creep in. And then you came." Vin looked up, that same frown returning. (p268)

11 | Examples of third-person pronouns

If you are commissioned to work on a novel with gender-neutral pronouns, talk to your author about the following:

- Whether the pronoun use is normative but gender-neutral or identity-based.
- If it's identity-based, whether they've considered the viewpoint implications.
- Which pronouns should be used and how they should be conjugated according to case.

There are many variations and the mindful editor is encouraged to check rather than assume the spelling.

Here are some examples, some of which you'll be familiar with, others perhaps not so much.

Subjective pronoun	Objective pronoun	Possessive adjective/ possessive determiner	Possessive pronoun	Reflexive pronoun
Ey is an editor	I like **em**	**Eir** job is interesting	That pen is **eirs**	Ey doubts **emself**
It is an editor	I like **it**	**Its** job is interesting	That pen is **its**	It doubts **itself**
Ne is an editor	I like **nem**	**Nir** job is interesting	That pen is **nirs**	Ne doubts **nemself**
Per is an editor	I like **per**	**Per** job is interesting	That pen is **pers**	Per doubts **perself**
She is an editor	I like **her**	**Her** job is interesting	That pen is **hers**	She doubts **herself**
They are an editor	I like **them**	**Their** job is interesting	That pen is **theirs**	They doubt **themselves/ themself**
Thon is an editor	I like **thon**	**Thons** job is interesting	That pen is **thons**	Thon doubts **thonself**
Ve is an editor	I like **ver**	**Vis** job is interesting	That pen is **vis**	Ve doubts **verself**
Xe is an editor	I like **xem**	**Xyr** job is interesting	That pen is **xyrs**	Xe doubts **xemself**
Ze is an editor	I like **zir**	**Zir** job is interesting	That pen is **zirs**	Ze doubts **zirself**
Ze is an editor	I like **zem**	**Zer** job is interesting	That pen is **zers**	Ze doubts **zemself**
Ze is an editor	I like **hir**	**Hir** job is interesting	That pen is **hirs**	Ze doubts **hirself**

12 | Tracking characters' pronouns

Use a style sheet to track characters' chosen pronouns in the same way you'd keep track of other distinguishing features such as hair and skin colour, height and weight, personality traits and other distinguishing features that must be consistent.

If your author's using identity-based pronouns that hold viewpoint, you'll need to record not only characters' personal choices but also what pronouns they use for others when they're narrating as a viewpoint character.

13 | Can fiction include a mixture of gendered and gender-neutral pronouns?

Fiction can absolutely include a mixture of gendered and gender-neutral pronouns.

In English, normative approaches to writing already use a mixture of pronouns. Moving beyond the binary just increases the number of options in the pot.

The difference is that normative approaches use gendered pronouns that are based on audiovisual, behavioural and touch-based perceptions – *that person appears to be a man or sounds like a man so we'll* **prescribe** *the pronouns 'he' and 'him'*. They're objective.

Just like people in the real world, the characters in a novel have distinct identities and preferences about the language used about them. A character's pronouns are theirs to choose and use as they want, which means they might opt for 'they', 'she', 'he', 'xe', 've', 'per' or something else, regardless of whether they're cis, trans or non-binary.

Just bear in mind the viewpoint implications when you're editing.

14 | Should writers include explanations?

What should you do if your author asks for advice on whether to explain why they've included a character with a gender-neutral pronoun? There's no right or wrong approach.

Centring character

On the one hand, if their intention is to centre character rather than their pronoun usage, an explanation of why they've written characters with gender-neutral pronouns runs the risk of the very othering they're trying to avoid.

My bookshelves are crowded with fictional worlds inhabited by cisgendered characters with binary pronouns, and there are a few with trans characters also with binary pronouns. Not one of them includes an explanation from the author about why they chose to gender their characters as they did nor why those characters are referred to as 'he' or 'she'.

If writers want to disrupt rather than enforce normative ideas about identity, playing by the same invisibilisation rules in regard to explanation could make sense.

Centring marginalisation

On the other hand, your author might want to make a statement or a call for readers to actively reimagine the way people are identified by others in the dominant culture.

In *Beyond Binary*, editor Brit Mandelo devotes an introductory chapter to why they created an anthology of speculative fiction stories featuring sexually fluid and genderqueer characters, some of whom use gender-neutral pronouns and some, binary pronouns.

Pronunciation and information

Readers might not be aware of how to pronounce some of the pronouns in the novel. In that case, brief guidance would increase engagement.

An alternative could be to focus not on the *why* but on the *that*. There's a precedent for this approach in some editions of Arnaldur Indriðason's *Jar City* – a note about Icelandic names and why first names are used even when criminals and police address each other. The issue is different but the intention is the same – to educate readers.

And so perhaps you might best serve your author by talking through the various options and helping them discover the best path for their book.

15 | Summing up

Editing fiction that uses non-gendered pronouns needs to be approached with a mindfulness that reaches beyond consistency.

Discuss your author's preferences for spelling, and track each character's identity traits if the fictional universe you're editing is written in a third-person narration style and allows for multiple pronoun choices.

An understanding of viewpoint is critical, as is careful reflection on the degree to which a viewpoint character consciously de-genders their own language because of where they are on the conscious-language spectrum.

And don't forget that by helping your clients understand how grammar, identity and writing craft intersect, you'll be serving their stories and their readers.

16 | Resources

Armstrong, SL (2012). *Gender neutral pronouns in fiction*. Storm Moon Press. **stormmoonpress.wordpress.com/2012/04/28/gender-neutral-pronouns-in-fiction**

Griffiths, E (2015). *The Ghost Fields*. Quercus.

Harnby, L. *An Introduction to Narrative Point of View*, multimedia course. **louiseharnbyproofreader.com/pov-workshop.html**

Harnby, L (2020). *Editing Fiction at Sentence Level*. Panx Press. **louiseharnbyproofreader.com/editing-fiction-at-sentence-level.html**

Harnby, L (2020). *Making Sense of Point of View*. Panx Press. **louiseharnbyproofreader.com/making-sense-of-point-of-view.html**

Harnby, L (2021). *Making Sense of 'Show, Don't Tell'*. Panx Press. **louiseharnbyproofreader.com/making-sense-of-show-dont-tell.html**

Indriðason, A (2009). *Jar City*. Vintage.

McCarthy, C (2009). *The Road*. Picador.

Mandelo, B, ed. (2012). *Beyond Binary*. Lethe Press.

Mardell, A (2016). *The ABC's of LGBT+*. Mango.

Queer Little Family (2020). Pronouns 101. **queerlittlefamily.co.uk/pronouns101**

Safe Zone Project. LGBTQ+ vocabulary: Glossary of terms. **thesafezoneproject.com/resources/vocabulary**

Saller, C (2021). Gender-neutral pronouns in creative writing. CMOS Shop Talk. **cmosshoptalk.com/2021/04/20/gender-neutral-pronouns-in-creative-writing**

Sullivan, M (2014). *Hollow World*. Kindle edition. Tachyon Publications.

We Need Diverse Books (2020). The rise of gender-inclusive pronouns and language in literature.
diversebooks.org/the-rise-of-gender-inclusive-pronouns-and-language-in-literature

Western Oregon University. Preferred gender pronoun/personal pronouns.
wou.edu/wp/safezone/pronoun

Zusak, M (2016). *The Book Thief*. Definitions.

Appendix | Summary of narrative viewpoint styles

The table in this appendix summarises the most commonly used narration styles the fiction editor is likely to encounter and what the limitations are in terms of what can be reported to the reader.

All the examples use traditional pronouns. The intention is not to erase gender identity or ignore neopronouns but to centre the learning in this appendix on narrative style and what the reader can access.

Bear in mind that skilled writers can blend third-person limited, objective and omniscient narrative styles together.

Appendix | Summary of narrative viewpoint styles

Narrative style	Pronouns	Internal experience	External events and behaviour
First person	I, we	Readers can access only the internal, subjective experience of the 'I' narrator, for example thoughts, emotions, identity. They have no access to what's going on in the heads of other characters. Examples • The leaves are speckled with a red dust that I can't identify. What the hell is that stuff? • I can't help myself. I'm furious with her. • I'm confident in my masculinity, despite my vulva and breasts.	Readers can access only what the 'I' narrator can objectively perceive, for example sound, landscape, speech, movement. Examples • My friend snorted and spat tea onto the ground. • The leaves were speckled with red dust. • 'I'm fed up with your relentless sarcasm,' Stan said. • Stan wiped spittle from his mouth and shook his head.

Narrative style	Pronouns	Internal experience	External events and behaviour
Second person	You	Readers can access only the internal, subjective experience of the 'you' viewpoint character, for example thoughts, emotions, identity. They have no access to what's going on in the heads of other characters. Examples - The leaves are speckled with a red dust that you can't identify. What the hell is that stuff? - You can't help yourself. You're furious with her. - You're confident in your masculinity, despite your vulva and breasts.	Readers can access only what the 'you' viewpoint character can objectively perceive, for example sound, landscape, speech, movement. Examples - Your friend snorted and spat tea onto the ground. - The leaves were speckled with red dust. - 'I'm fed up with your relentless sarcasm,' Stan said. - Stan wiped spittle from his mouth and shook his head.

Appendix | Summary of narrative viewpoint styles

Narrative style	Pronouns	Internal experience	External events and behaviour
Third-person limited	She, he, it, they, ze, per +	Readers can access only the internal, subjective experience of the viewpoint character, for example thoughts, emotions, identity. They have no access to what's going on in the heads of other characters. Examples • The leaves are speckled with a red dust that she can't identify. What the hell is that stuff? • He can't help himself. He's furious with her. • He's confident in his masculinity, despite his vulva and breasts.	Readers can access only what the viewpoint character can objectively perceive, for example sound, landscape, speech, movement. Examples • Her friend snorted and spat tea onto the ground. • The leaves were speckled with red dust. • 'I'm fed up with your relentless sarcasm,' Stan said. • Stan wiped spittle from his mouth and shook his head.

Narrative style	Pronouns	Internal experience	External events and behaviour
Third-person objective	She, he, it, they, ze, per +	Readers have no access to any character's internal, subjective experience.	Readers can access only what can be objectively perceived, for example sound, landscape, speech, movement. *Examples* <ul><li>The green jumper hangs off Lee's almost skeletal frame. He stoops under the doorway, trips, finds his feet and heads to the bar.</li><li>The old bell chimes right on time but it's barely audible through the din of the crowd.</li><li>The leaves were speckled with red dust.</li><li>'I'm fed up with your relentless sarcasm,' Stan said.</li></ul>

Appendix | Summary of narrative viewpoint styles

Narrative style	Pronouns	Internal experience	External events and behaviour
Third-person omniscient	I, we, you, she, he, it, they, ze, per +	Readers have full access to any and every character's internal, subjective experience via the godlike narrator. Example • Little Lou. The moniker has been in play since the day they were born. Our poor Lou detests the diminution, though never lets on for fear of offending Mama, who is of a delicate disposition. A pity since Mama secretly can't abide the name either but is damned if she'll admit it.	Readers can access anything that can be objectively perceived by anyone, anywhere via the godlike narrator. Example • The black Alfa parks on French Street at 14:52 precisely. Three blocks down, an identical car slips into the parking bay opposite the market. Twenty miles east of the city, the phone rings. The reckoning has begun and by tomorrow morning it is all anyone will be talking about.

About the author

Louise Harnby is a professional fiction editor who specialises in working with independent crime, thriller and mystery writers. She is an Advanced Professional Member of the CIEP and has been working with words for 30 years.

She offers a suite of books and training courses that help editors develop their marketing and business skills and hone their line craft, particularly in relation to commercial fiction. She also cohosts The Editing Podcast with Denise Cowle.

harnby.co/fiction-editing

Acknowledgements

Many thanks to Sophie Playle, Nick Taylor, Ian Howe, Luke Finley and Margaret Hunter, who reviewed the draft of this guide for sense and sensibility. I'm grateful for their mindful advice and comments.

Thanks also to Cathy Tingle for her warm and professional management of this project. An editorial ship runs oh so smoothly when Cathy's at the helm.

And, finally, a special mention for my pal, business-accountability partner and fellow podcaster Denise Cowle. Together, we get stuff done and make it fun!

Louise Harnby
September 2021

www.ingramcontent.com/pod-product-compliance
Lightning Source LLC
Chambersburg PA
CBHW070104120526
44588CB00034B/2314